Maggie Ross Irish Step

By Ann Cothran Kallal   Coloring Book

MaggieRossDance.com

Come visit our website to see these and many other unique designs in
a variety of hair and costume colors on products for Dancers including
Teacher and Dance Mother designs. Personalization is easy to accomplish
using our Text Tool. Buy with confidence on clothing, novelty and gift items.

Created from my original artwork. Unconditionally guaranteed.

4

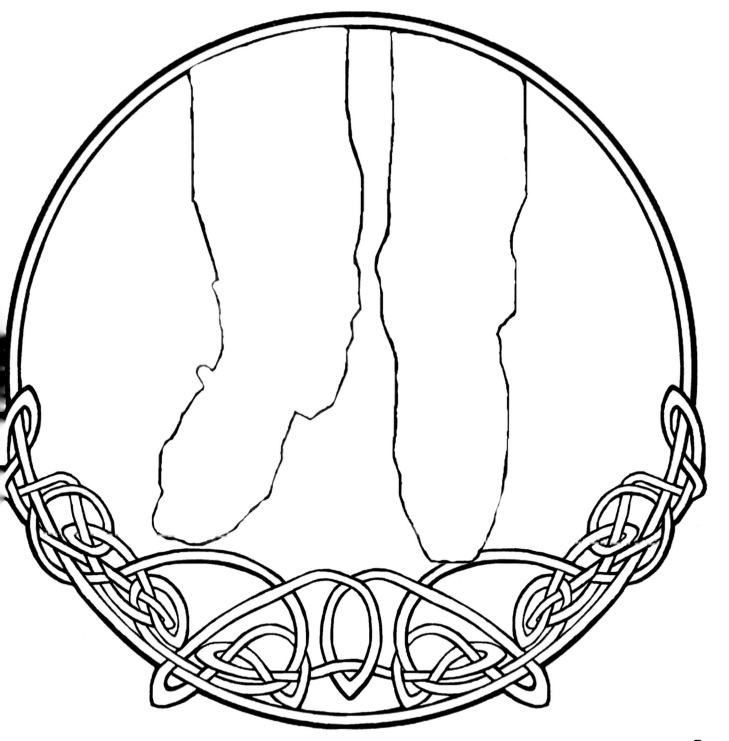

5

ann
©'16
MaggieRossDance.com

MaggieRossDance.com

ann ©'16
MaggieRossDance.com

ann ©'16
MaggieRossDance.com

17

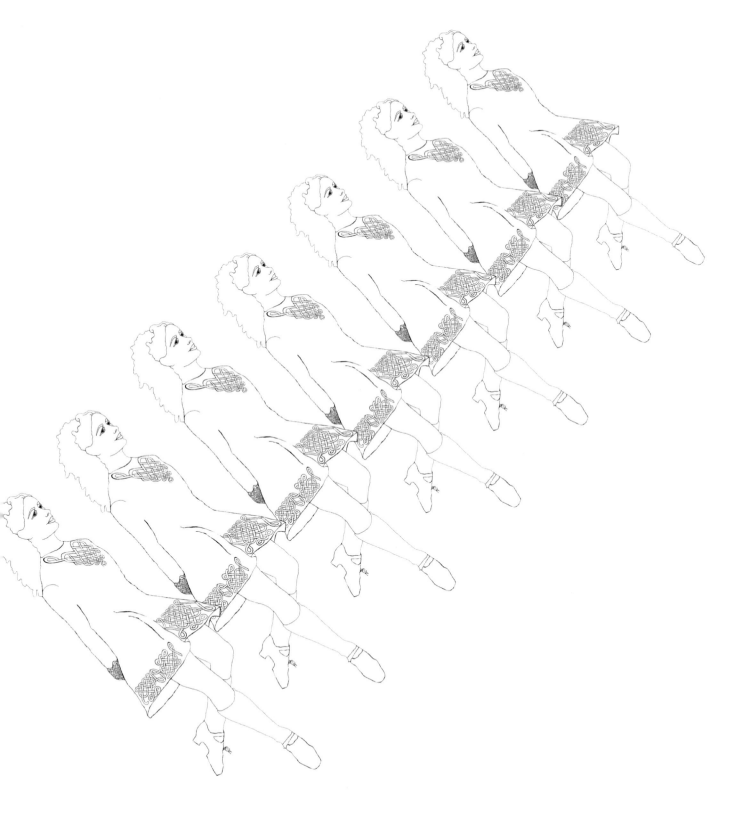

ann
©'16
MaggieRossDance.com

ann
©'16
MaggieRossDance.com

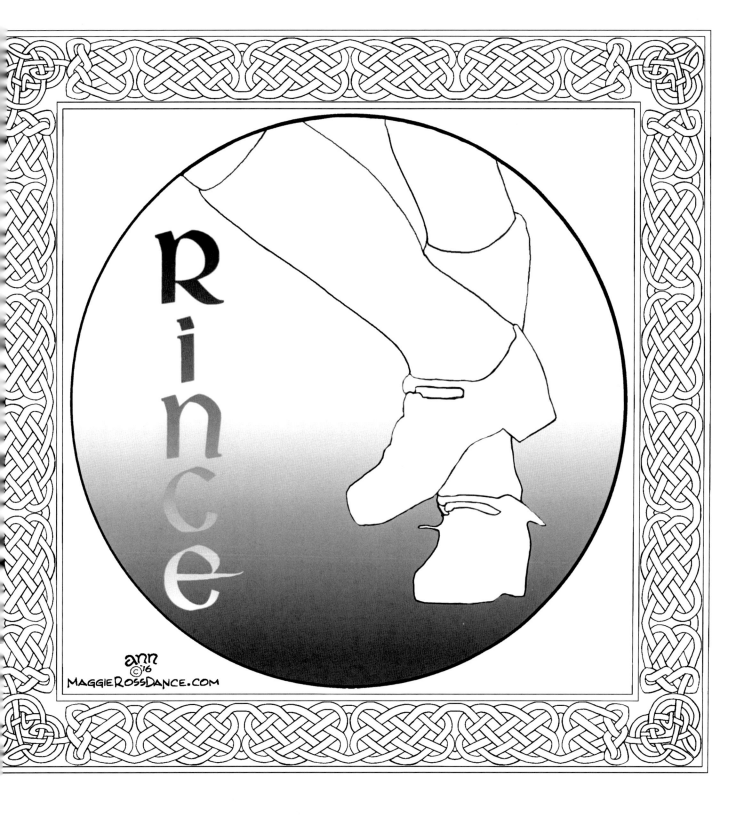

IRISH DANCER

ann ©'16
MaggieRossDance.com

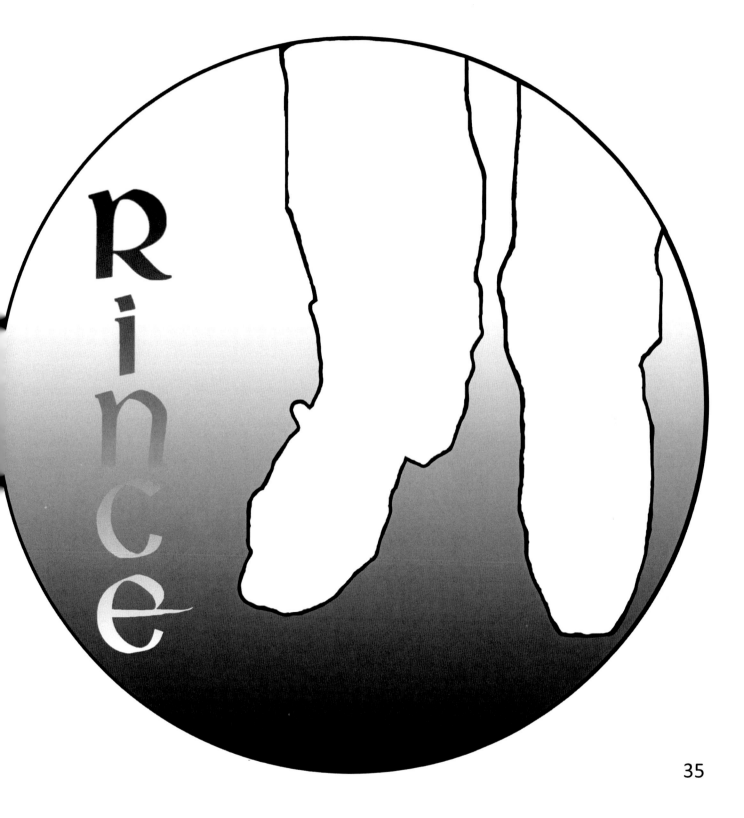

Irish
Dance
Teacher

Irish Dance Teacher

IRISH DANCE

TEACHER

ann ©'16
MaggieRossDance.co[m]

irish dance

teacher

42

43

Irish
Dance
Mother

ann
©'16
MaggieRossDance.com

44

Irish
Dance
Mother

IRISh DANCE

mother

ann©'16
MaggieRossDance.com

irish dance

mother

'Dance, then, wherever you may be;
I am the Lord of the Dance,' said he;
'And I'll lead you all, wherever you may be,
I will lead you all in the Dance,' said he.

S. Carter

Bibliographic Note

Maggie Ross Irish Stepdance Coloring Book is a new work.
The designs were created from my original artwork which
is for sale online on clothing, novelty and gift items. Come
visit our website: http://www.MaggieRossDance.com

International Standard Book Number
ISBN-13: 978-1532936395
ISBN-10: 1532936397

Manufactured in the United States of America

Made in the
USA
Middletown, DE